For Pamela Freer

Owen Morrel

Works 1976-1984

Introduction
by Trent Myers

Madison Art Center, Madison, Wisconsin
September 30–November 25, 1984

Contemporary Arts Museum, Houston, Texas
January 26–March 17, 1984

Organized by the Madison Art Center with the aid of a grant from the National Endowment for the Arts, Washington, D.C., and with additional support from the 1984-1985 Exhibition Underwriters of the Madison Art Center.

Lenders to the Exhibition

Louis Gaudiosi, New York
Mr. and Mrs. Scott Hodes, Chicago
Owen Morrel
Charles L. Zarett, New York
Anonymous

Library of Congress Card No. N6537.M648A4
ISBN 0-913883123

Designed by: Mixed Media, Madison, WI
Typeset by: KC Graphics, Madison, WI
Printed by: Park Printing, Ltd., Verona, WI
2000 copies printed in September, 1984.

Cover: *McGraw-Hill Rising,* 1981 (Cat. No. 28)

Preface and Acknowledgments

The idea for a small Owen Morrel exhibition first arose in a casual conversation I had several years ago with Scott Hodes, a Chicago attorney who represents a number of artists and who is a collector of contemporary art. I corresponded with Hodes and the artist about the show, but the project had to wait until the arrival of Trent Myers as Curator of Exhibitions two years ago to really get underway. It was a felicitous relationship, for the idea of a Morrel show had already been brewing in Trent's mind for some time. Visits to Owen's studio in New York soon convinced us that there was enough work of such quality and diversity available that a much larger show than we originally envisioned was justified. Owen's reputation is based on his work as a sculptor; we found that he was an accomplished draftsman, photographer and maker of collages as well. It is hoped that this exhibition will give a more rounded picture of his accomplishments.

Working with Owen has been a stimulating experience for Trent and for the Art Center. The artist possesses an abundant energy that is usually channeled into creating works of art, and his excitement for his work is infectious. He has responded to all our requests for information and photographs with the same enthusiasm that he puts into his work. In the interviews with Trent Myers on which the catalog essay is based, he was thoughtful, articulate, and obviously very involved in what he's doing.

Many individuals have assisted with various aspects of the exhibition, and on behalf of the Board of Trustees and the staff, I warmly thank them. The lenders to the exhibition, listed elsewhere in this catalog, have generously agreed to part with their works for the nine month period while the show is in Madison and at the Contemporary Arts Museum in Houston, Texas. It also gives me great pleasure to acknowledge those who have contributed financial support for the exhibition: Scott Hodes, and James J. Pelts of Chicago. Betsy Cohn, Owen's assistant, has been helpful in assembling information for the catalog. Shalom Gorewitz has made videotapes of Owen's work available for the exhibition. Others who have assisted in important ways are Philip Angell, John Birmingham, Janice DeBerry, Brooke Larsen, and Harriet and Melvin Morrel. I also want to thank the people of Malleable Metals, Bethany, Connecticut: Phyllis Cummings, Robert Giza, Fran Patnaude, Gary Staffa, Robert Stanford, and Peter Verteeg.

Special thanks are due to members of the Madison Art Center staff who have worked on various aspects of the exhibition and catalog. Trent Myers has organized the exhibition and written an insightful essay for the catalog. Janet Ela, Curator of Collections, generously contributed her talents as an editor in revising the catalog manuscript. Bob Schroeder, Registrar, orchestrated shipping and receiving of all works of art. The exhibition was installed by Bill Lindemann, Technical Services Supervisor, and his staff, Barry Carlsen and Royce Weatherly. Louise Weinberg handled research, proof-reading, and verification of details relating to the catalog, while Gwen Winston was responsible for producing the manuscript. Diane Fellows made photographs of the installation and for publicity.

The catalog was designed by Nancy Zucker of Mixed Media. Catalog photographs were supplied by Owen Morrel and Maurice Thaler.

I would also like to thank Natasha Nicholson for support at the time of the opening.

The exhibition was organized with the aid of a grant from the National Endowment for the Arts, Washington, D.C.
Additional support was received from the 1984-85 Exhibition Underwriters of the Madison Art Center:
American of Madison
Carley Capital Group
CUNA Mutual Insurance Society
Marshall Erdman & Associates
Oscar Mayer Company
Webcrafters, Inc.

Thomas H. Garver
Director

Introduction

I'm angry with the degeneration of perception, with the place where people's minds go for safety. Society imposes a set of conditionings on our minds, and I'm fighting to break out of that, to discover things the way they really are, not as we're conditioned to assume they are.—Owen Morrel[1]

An interest in the physiological and psychological aspects of perception has been a current that has run through much of the sculpture made over the past two decades. Accompanying this has been a radical questioning of the nature of sculpture, and an expansion of its boundaries as a category: no longer does a sculpture need to be an object looked at from without, existing in its own idealized space and separated from the real world by the mediating function of its pedestal. Of course, the pedestal had been gradually disappearing since the advent of modernism; with the arrival of minimalism in the 1960s, it had all but vanished.[2] Yet this development did not stop there; in the seventies the discrete sculptural object itself become more and more difficult to locate as it was replaced by earthworks, site-specific works, scatter pieces, interior installations involving many separate visual components, and a host of other manifestations.

Much of this new work was participatory: viewers moved through or stood within a piece, so that their experience of it was kinesthetic as well as visual. Wanting to exploit the possibilities of the changed relationship between viewer and work, many sculptors began to focus on perceptual issues—how sense data are organized by our minds, and how perceptions are shaped by cultural factors. The work of Robert Irwin and James Turrell springs immediately to mind in this regard. Other artists constructing participatory works have been interested in leading viewers through a set of experiences designed to elicit specific psychological responses. Alice Aycock's *A Simple Network of Underground Wells and Tunnels,* 1975, for example, was an interconnected series of underground spaces, through which viewers had to crawl and drop to a slightly lower level wherever a tunnel intersected one of the vertical shafts of the wells. Three of the wells were open to daylight, and three were closed over, so the viewer/participant was forced to move alternately toward and away from the light.

It is now beginning to be understood just what these developments mean: in works that require a high degree of viewer participation, the locus of creative subjectivity is shifted away from the artist and toward the spectator. An artist who constructs a participatory work does not so much "express" him or herself as create a context within which one must act for there to be "art." Up to a certain point the artist has control; after that, the responsibility belongs to the viewer, and in many cases, there is a great deal of latitude for individual responses. Sculpture in this "expanded field"[3] violates a fundamental premise of the modernist credo: that the work of art first and foremost embodies the artist's privileged vision of reality, and that the work exists to communicate that vision to a more or less passive recipient.

It is in the context of these developments that we must place the work of Owen Morrel. Morrel is known primarily for seven ambitious environmental sculptures he has conceived and executed since 1976. Four of these works have been dismantled: *Telescopic Reference Points,* 1976; *Desk Axis,* 1976; *Catapult 70°,* 1977; and *Asylum,* 1978. Three are extant: *Omega,* 1980; *Boomerang,* 1981; and the recently installed *Pilot Bridge,* 1984. Each has been concerned with perception, specifically with freeing vision from cultural influences, and each has required the active participation of the viewer. Morrel does not design his sculptures simply to be looked at, although they have all been quite rewarding in a purely visual sense. Rather, one looks out instead of in: all have involved climbing to a designated observation platform where one's attention is diverted away from the work itself and out toward the surrounding environment. The views could be quite spectacular, for most of the sculptures were sited in high places: *Desk Axis, Catapult 70°,* and *Asylum* on rooftops in New York City; *Omega* cantilevered out over a gorge of the Niagra river; and *Boomerang* extending out from a skyscraper setback, thirty-three stories up.

Reaching the observation platform of a Morrel sculpture involves progressively abandoning one's ingrained perceptual baggage. Built into each piece are elements that undermine our visual habits in ways that are sometimes subtle, but more often are dramatic or even sensational. Ultimately one loses awareness of the piece itself, and begins to see the surrounding world through new eyes, unencumbered by an imposed way of seeing that has been learned over a lifetime. The important thing to remember is that the viewer is always at the center of the work: "I do not put the works on pedestals," says Morrel, "I put people on pedestals."

That the sculptures have been successful in expanding the possibilites of visual perception is shown by the fact that they have led Morrel to widen the scope of his art to include other media: drawings, photographs, and photo-collages. Although many of these two-dimensional works are associated with one or another of the sculptural projects, very few can be considered studies or the kind of documentation one usually associates with site-specific pieces. The drawings are too finely crafted to be merely the working out of sculptural ideas; they are independent works in themselves, every bit as meaningful, albeit in a different way, as the sculpture. In the photographs and photo-collages, a sculpture will often appear only to serve as a point of reference. In a photo-collage from 1981 (Cat. No. 27), for example, *Boomerang* is barely visible near the top of the old McGraw-Hill building. The colliding planes and shifting viewpoints of the collage represent an attempt to intensify or explore in greater depth the sensations one might experience in relation to that particular sculpture. The function of the photographs and photo-collages is to focus and clarify concerns evolved initially in the sculpture. At the same time they allow Morrel to pursue these concerns independently of a major sculptural undertaking—an important consideration given the magnitude of the financial and logistical commitments such projects require.

Very little in Morrel's immediate background foreshadowed his first major project, *Telescopic Reference Points* (Cat. Nos. 1, 2), realized in the fall of 1976 near Poughkeepsie, New York. At Colgate University, Morrel studied creative writing and languages, and during a year at Skidmore, ceramics. This latter experience led him to become a potter for a brief period; he abandoned this direction soon after realizing he ''could not go beyond the objectness'' of his forms. He was interested in creating more open, fragile structures, and finding this impossible to do with clay, he turned to making wood and wire constructions. After he moved to New York City in 1973, he began doing environmental installations in his studio. Around 1975, he made several pieces using uprooted trees, whose trunks he drilled out and fitted with high-powered telescopes. These pieces became the basis for *Telescopic Reference Points.*

Installed on a large parcel of private land outside of Poughkeepsie, the work consisted of two components. The first was a steel mesh platform, about fifty feet off the ground, wrapped around the trunk of a hickory tree. One reached the platform by climbing a steel ladder affixed to the side of the tree. Once there, one looked through a telescope across a valley approximately a mile and a half to see an uprooted tree in a clearing. This was the second part of the work. After climbing down from the tree, one drove around the valley by car and walked through the woods to reach the uprooted tree. Behind it was a neatly excavated pit, in which one could sit to peer through an eyepiece embedded in the trunk. The eyepiece was connected to a periscopic telescope within the tree; through it one saw yet another location back across the valley, somewhat to the right of the original tree and platform.

The effect of the whole experience was to make one realize that the work as a whole was much grander in scale and conception than its two physical components, taken by themselves, initially suggested. One could not really ''get it'' until the very end, when it became clear that the work was actually a gigantic wedge of space defined by the sitelines of the telescopes. The sitelines theoretically could have been extended to infinity: thus the *true* scale of the work became beyond imagining.

In retrospect, *Telescopic Reference Points* appears to be a key work in Morrel's development: contained within it are elements that embody virtually the whole range of his later artistic concerns and aspirations. Important to its conception was what Morrel refers to as ''dismantling perception'': with causing spectators to go beyond their customary ways of seeing through an active involvement with the work. Climbing to an observation platform within the piece—the ''signature'' characteristic of a Morrel sculpture—and the sense of risk to personal safety this involved were central to the process. A willingness to take such a risk was a precondition for the liberation of vision experienced on the platform. There, spectators might have felt a tinge of acrophobia accompanied at the same time by the exhilaration of being able to literally ''see farther'': in a sense to feel the extension of their bodies out over the landscape. In *Telescopic Reference Points,* the telescopes made this sense of extension a literal and purely optical experience. In later works, Morrel would use mirrors for the same purpose, but more effectively, since the view wasn't limited to what could be seen through an eyepiece.

Telescopic Reference Points was followed in rapid succession by two works of decidedly different character. Whereas the earlier piece was basically ''abstract,'' not unlike much of the environmental work being done in the mid-70s, *Desk Axis,* 1976 (Cat. No. 4), and *Catapult 70°*, 1977 (Cat. No. 6), initially must have seemed like capricious surrealist pranks. Both were based on the use of found objects, which in the context of their placement, took a host of associations and gave Morrel's art a new metaphorical dimension. *Telescopic Reference Points* was concerned more purely with perceptual psychology; in the new pieces, Morrel broadened his interest to encompass the sociology of perception as well. Specifically, he was interested in the influence of cultural factors on the way we see.

Desk Axis grew out of a number of things Morrel had been thinking about around the time he completed *Telescopic Reference Points.* He had grown up on Long Island, where his parents had a home on the water. The sea had been an integral part of his childhood, and its horizontal expansiveness, his being able to see the horizon as a continuous line, made a strong impression on him. On moving to New York, he was struck by the contrast between the city's verticality and his own psychological orientation to the horizontal: ''The first thing that really hit me was the feeling of closure, of existing in canyons, and not being able to see the horizon or the sun go down.'' To get back to the horizontal, Morrel began to spend an increasing amount of time on the roof of the building in Brooklyn where he had a loft. The building was somewhat higher than those immediately around it, so the roof afforded good views of Manhattan just across the East River. Morrel found the roof a good place to get away and think, write, and reflect on the direction of his art. It also gave him an opportunity to see the city as a totality, to not be encompassed by it without understanding how it affected him and its other inhabitants psychologically. The vertical, geometric structure of the city—as exemplified in its skyline—came to symbolize for him rational thought and the kind of psychic repression necessitated by living in an orderly society. On the other hand, the sky and the horizontal came to symbolize unfettered psychological freedom. At the same time these ideas were coming together in Morrel's mind, he was also spending a lot of time drawing at an old desk someone had left behind in his loft. Eventually he got the idea of taking the desk up to the roof, and out of this *Desk Axis* was born.

To make the piece, Morrel mounted the desk and a swivel chair on a twelve foot high steel tripod, and installed the whole ensemble on the roof. Metal rungs were affixed to the tripod so that one could climb up and sit in the chair. In the top center of the desk was an opening through which one could see into the eyepiece of a periscopic telescope mounted internally within the desk. The telescope was aimed not straight ahead, but to one's left, toward the Statue of Liberty some three miles distant; peering through the eyepiece one saw the statue sideways.

Morrel could not have chosen a more apt metaphor to express his conern with perceptual and psychological freedom. The desk embodied for him all his distrust for the rational, regimented ways of thinking he associated with urban society: ''Consciously, I was aware that the desk symbolized rational thinking, the work ethic, '9-to-5', routine, and the social conditioning that routine and the workaday world imposes on our minds.'' The idea of sitting at a desk that is apparently floating weightlessly above the rooftops is a fantasy that should appeal to desk-bound office workers everywhere. What made *Desk Axis* so compelling was that it was much more than a mere representation of this fantasy: for those willing to take the risk, there was the opportunity to actually live it out.

Experiencing the work involved the subversion of one's expectations and the discovery of visual surprises at each step of the way. First was the sight of the desk and chair themselves in fantastic juxtaposition with the sky. After mounting the work, one's balance—and sense of security—was likely to be thrown off, since neither the desk nor chair were horizontal, but tilted a few degrees from the horizontal. Finally, looking through the eyepiece did not reveal anything within the desk, but something that was several miles away, and in a direction contrary to the way one was looking. The image itself, like the desk and chair, was tilted away from a horizontal-vertical orientation. The combined effect of all these elements was to induce visual disorientation in the spectator, to play havoc with one's perceptual apparatus; Morrel admits that the piece was somewhat ''anarchistic'' in this way. Yet after getting over the initial disorientation, one was likely to feel an exhilarating sensation of freedom; a feeling reinforced by the sly incorporation of the Statue of Liberty into the work's imagery. The piece literally gave one the ability to see with new eyes, to view things from an unconstrained point of view.

Catapult 70°, realized in the spring of 1977, built upon ideas which had their genesis in *Desk Axis.* The piece was similar in conception to the earlier work, consisting of a psychoanalyst's couch and chair mounted on a steel tripod that was installed on a rooftop in Manhattan. It also included a telescope, which like the one in *Desk Axis* was periscopic, so the view was always at an angle to the direction one was looking. The eyepiece of the telescope was set into the center of a circular mirror. A steel ladder enabled one to climb the tripod and lie on the couch. By facing the mirror just to the right, one confronted a collision of viewpoints. Reflected in the mirror were one's own face and upper torso, part of the chair, and the landscape behind it. This image was ''punctured'' by another contradictory one: that which could be seen through the eyepiece of the telescope. The base of the tripod was attached to a circular track, so the whole work could be revolved through 360°, resulting in even greater visual dissonance at the edge where the two vistas ran together.

What Morrel accomplished in *Catapult 70°* was, as he puts it, ''to juggle the order of one's perceptions, to dismantle them so that they might be reassembled from a new point of view.'' The desire to alter perception again was related to Morrel's dissatisfaction with the ''institutionalization'' of consciousness, that is, with the invisible, unrelenting pressures by which society and its institutions shape the way we see and think:

> *I chose a psychoanalyst's couch and chair because they seemed to represent all the paternalistic relations between an individual and society: government—in the guise of big brother—education, and even religion, are all in a way father figures. I wanted to subvert these relationships in which we give up responsibility for our own actions, and give the power of decision-making back to the viewer.*

Seen in this context, the use of the trappings of psychoanalysis in *Catapult 70°* acquires a double meaning. The interaction between patient and analyst can be viewed as a paternalistic relationship *par excellance.* The patient, to an extent, surrenders the autonomy of his or her mental life to the analyst; the analyst, in turn, acts as a guide, comforter, judge, in short, as a ''father'' (although certainly one should not take this notion too far—most analysts would argue that this characterization is a perversion of the psychoanalytic process). On the other hand, in a more positive sense, the psychoanalyst's couch is also a place of therapy, a place to attain new insights into the self and one's relationship to others and the world. *Catapult 70°,* the psychoanalyst's couch in the sky, was such a therapeutic place, where the viewer/patient could break free of societal influences and begin a return to a more innocent state of being.

Asylum, 1978 (Cat. No. 10), was Morrel's first piece constructed entirely to his own design that did not utilize found objects: he describes it as his first leap into abstraction. At the time he conceived it, he was beginning to think that *Desk Axis* and *Catapult 70°* were too literal: that their specificity as objects limited the free rein of imagination. He also had been thinking about the opposing concepts of imprisonment and freedom; he realized that all human beings are imprisoned within their own bodies, and that their desire to transcend their physical nature is embodied in the basic human impulse toward flight. *Asylum* would give form to the conflict between, on the one hand, our awareness of our corporal limits, and on the other, our desire for transcendence, by presenting the somewhat paradoxical image of a prison in the sky. The title of the work actually preceded the design: the word itself has conflicting meanings which express the dichotomy Morrel wanted to convey. In one sense, asylum means a place of refuge, a location where one can go to escape the constraints of society. Yet the word also harbors a nearly opposite, more sinister meaning: in a now out-of-date usage, asylum could mean "insane asylum," an institution where the mentally ill, that is, those incapable of living according to socially established norms, were sent for incarceration.

Asylum was installed on the roof of the American Thread Building in lower Manhattan. An open, cage-like structure formed the major part of the work. Two sides of the cage were closed in with prison bars salvaged from a demolished west side penitentiary. A third side had only a horizontal railing. Opposite that was a mirrored wall fitted with a standardized, sliding prison door. The mirror was tipped back a few degrees to reflect the sky. There was no roof, and the floor was an open metal grid. The cage, twenty-four feet above the building's roof, rested on a metal scaffold, and was reached by three flights of stairs.

The use of a large mirror in *Asylum* marked an important development in Morrel's work. Henceforth, he would use mirrors in the same way he had used telescopes in the earlier pieces: as a means to suggest the extension of the viewer's body out over the environment surrounding the piece. He had come to a point where he realized telescopes were ultimately inadequate for this task, since they really involved only the eye. By contrast, large mirrors incorporated the whole body and everything around it, and made things appear in locations they did not actually occupy. In effect, they visually "displaced" the objects they reflected.

Those who ascended the stairs to the cage in *Asylum* were able to experience the contradictions embodied in the title. Standing on the open grid floor, one could almost imagine oneself floating above the rooftop. The sensation of being detached from the earth was reinforced by perceptual clues Morrel built into the piece. None of the walls met at right angles, and even the floor had a pronounced tilt. One wanted to think one was within a perfect cube; that would have been the normal, rational—that is to say, conditioned—response. Yet one's expectations were continually frustrated, and a slight case of spatial disorientation was the likely result. The "cube" one imagined to be in must have seemed as if it were coming apart, or alternatively, as if it were wrenching itself loose from the scaffold prior to drifting away in the sky. Yet, one could not get too carried away by the experience. The prison bars and door, as well as the sturdy scaffold visible beneath the floor, served as reminders that one is ultimately earthbound, a prisoner of gravity. One only had to open the door and descend the stairs to come down.

Morrel's first three major sculptural projects had all been temporary installations; in 1980 he finally had an opportunity to construct his first major, semi-permanent work when the Parks Department of New York State commissioned him to do a piece at Artpark, a publicly funded park devoted to the fine arts in Lewiston, New York. *Omega* (Cat. No. 15), as the piece was titled, took nearly two years to realize. It is perhaps Morrel's most monumental work, and along with *Pilot Bridge,* his most publicly accessible.

As in *Asylum,* the title preceded and in part determined the form of *Omega.* On Morrel's first trip to Artpark to scout possible locations for the new work, he decided on its basic structure:

> *On my way, I was reading a book called* Time, Space and Knowledge, *by Tarthang Tulku. I was also thinking about David Smith, about "Terminal Iron Works," about the word "terminal" with its implications of juncture, an ending, a place where things meet and depart at the same time. I wrote the word in my book and forgot it for the moment . . . . On the way home, I wrote down the word "Omega," and drew a small Omega symbol, the round one with funny little feet at the ends. That night, I did a small drawing and chopped off the corners of the Omega with mirrors.*[4]

The final appearance of *Omega* does not differ significantly from the initial sketch. Its structure consists of two long, open-grate catwalks cantilivered out over the Niagra River, some 200 feet below. These are linked at one end of the work by a third catwalk connected to a series of stairways. At the far end of *Omega,* the part that projects over the river, the catwalks converge and terminate in twin look-out platforms. Three large mirrors are positioned around the platforms: one beneath each of the platforms and one overhead in the space between them. The entire structure is supported on two asymmetric legs resting on two massive stone piers—all that remains of a nineteenth century suspension bridge that originally spanned the river at the site. As one would expect, there are few right angles in the work, and no level surface to stand on. The structure is pitched seven degrees both vertically and horizontally—just enough to send participants instinctively grasping for the handrail. Overall, *Omega* has a delicate, graceful appearance; despite its forty-ton weight, it appears almost feather light in comparison with the stone piers on which it rests. Indeed, it almost resembles a giant, yet fragile, insect, ready at any moment to rise up and walk away. The title of the work is a clue to the nature of the experience. Omega, the word, is the final letter of the Greek alphabet, and means terminus, the end point of any series or process. Corresponding to this definition, *Omega,* the sculpture, is like a terminus that is a jumping off point for fresh perceptual insights; it is both an ending and beginning. As one proceeds up one of the catwalks towards the platform and mirrors, the open-grate floor and angled surfaces have a disorienting effect. On reaching the platform, one has been prepared to adopt a new perspective, and the views to be had are not disappointing. Looking down, one sees oneself upside down, from the feet up, and because of the mirror's angle, apparently projected out in space over the river. Overhead, there is the reflected image of oneself standing on the platform, seemingly hovering over the river far below. The river and sky are inverted. The critic Sarah McFadden has written that the experience of watching oneself in the mirrors of *Omega* is like feeling the self gradually slip away, so that one becomes free to experience things in a new way.[5]

As the most ambitious project Morrel had undertaken thus far, *Omega* added a new dimension to the participatory aspects of his work. Previously, he had worked more or less on his own, using whatever casual help he could find. But the logistics of realizing *Omega* required planning and coordinating the efforts of a large group of people, and Morrel found himself working closely with structural engineers, steelworkers, architectural draftsmen, and other specialists. Morrel found that this process of collaboration paralleled what he was trying to do in his sculpture: to break down psychological barriers and expand awareness to accept new points of view. For Morrel and his collaborators, most of whom found themselves working on a project unlike any other they had known, this involved abandoning preconceived notions on the ''proper'' way of doing things, and opening themselves to new methodologies. Participation in the work, on this level, meant not an expansion of perception so much as an increased awareness of one's relationship to the ''totality'' of a collective activity. Of particular importance for Morrel was a concern with the way individuals place limits on their experience by focusing on only one aspect of a problem. He viewed the collaborative process of building *Omega* as an opportunity to deal with this issue: ''The increasing complexity of society has tended to isolate people within certain specialties, and in our specialization we have become isolated from each other. One of the functions I can serve as an artist is as an orchestrator, a person who brings together again people from various disciplines.''[6]

Beside the grandeur of *Omega,* Morrel's next piece, *Boomerang,* 1981 (Cat. No. 24), seems an almost modest gesture, but only on first sight. *Boomerang* is nearly hidden within the skyscraper canyons of central Manhattan; attached to the side of the old McGraw-Hill Building on West 42nd Street, it appears quite small from the street, overwhelmed by the vast scale of the surrounding architecture.

Built out from a setback, the major structural component of *Boomerang* is an arrow-shaped steel frame, whose point is directed out away from the building. A short flight of stairs leads from the building up through the lower arm of the frame to a small triangular platform positioned just above the point. Like the ones in *Asylum* and *Omega,* the platform is an open metal grid. Traversing the steel frame at a right angle and slanting back from the vertical is a V-shaped mirrored surface that vaguely resembles the boomerang of the title.

Boomerang works in a way that differs in one important respect from the earlier sculptures. With those pieces, the viewer could see what one was getting into beforehand: one saw the stairs and their terminus and thus was able to anticipate to some extent what the experience was going to be like. *Boomerang* allowed for no such anticipation; experiencing it was to feel a sudden visceral jolt, the perceptual equivalent of an electric shock. The approach to the work in no way prepares one for the experience; to the contrary, it tends to reinforce one's sense of security. From ground level, one enters an elevator, proceeds to the thirty-third floor, and walks down a corridor to a tiny utility room that serves as the access to the piece. So far, one has experienced only secure enclosed spaces, mostly windowless, and of course, all perfectly level vertically and horizontally. On passing through an opening in the wall of the utility room, one climbs the stairs to the platform of *Boomerang,* and finds oneself standing out in the open air, thirty-three stories above the street. The contrast between the confinement of the approach and the openness of the platform is felt immediately. One's knees feel weak, a knot forms in the stomach and a lump in the throat. The platform one stands on, naturally, is tilted, as if it were perversely calculated to up the stakes as one desperately tries to suppress acrophobia. Yet the views are truly spectacular. Far below, one can see the street; turn around and there is the mirror reflecting clouds and sky. Gradually, one's anxiety begins to subside, and the fear of falling gives way to a new, opposite sensation: the exhilaration of flight. One can imagine that one is at the controls of an airplane, or alternatively, standing in the bowsprit of an aerial sailboat.

The sensation of flying is really what *Boomerang* is all about, on the level of both metaphor and experience. The notion of flight also had informed *Asylum* and *Omega:* both of which in a sense were symbolic launching platforms for new perceptual experiences. The form of *Boomerang* alludes not just to the object referred to in its title, but to all kinds of flying phenomena: airplanes, kites, UFOs, the space shuttle, etc. As Morrel points out, the piece is "vehicular" on two levels: it evokes all these associations as well as carries viewers into new realms of experience. No doubt the clean, futuristic lines of *Boomerang* have a great deal to do with its ability to conjure up images connected with our space-age civilization. Yet one should not infer from this that Morrel has any special love for modern technology. "If anything," he says, "I use technology against itself." He views advanced technology with distrust, as representative of the sort of rational consciousness he wants to subvert in his work in favor of a more holistic way of thinking. As modern technology exerts an ever greater influence on our lives, Morrel is interested in turning the situation around, and placing individuals back in control. The image of *Boomerang* with someone standing on the platform—symbolically at the controls of the sculptural "vehicle"—could not be a more apt metaphor for this aspiration.

In many ways, *Pilot Bridge* (Cat. No. 35), installed in a small plaza on Franklin Street in lower Manhattan in the spring of 1984, represents a new departure for Morrel. It is his first free-standing work at ground level, and one in which the site does not play an important role. Perhaps most important is that Morrel has turned away from the "constructivist" idiom of his earlier sculpture; instead of relying on standardized industrial materials and structural elements, he has begun working with more open-ended, freely invented forms.

The turn in this direction was prompted by Morrel's desire to get away from what he refers to as the "literalness" of the earlier sculptures. He felt that in those works, the initial concept—and in the case of *Asylum* and *Omega,* the title—had to a large extent determined the form of the piece. He thought this strict adherence to the concept, the specificity with which a form referred to another thing or idea, ultimately limited what a work could "mean" to various observers. The forms of *Pilot Bridge,* Morrel notes, "are much more elusive." The piece consists of an open, lozenge-shaped structure mounted on three steel beams embedded in a granite boulder. Toward one end of the lozenge and passing through it is a shape vaguely resembling a taut bow. Wrapped around the steel beams is a staircase leading up into the work. The work is able to elicit many associations precisely because of its ambiguity; at any one time, one might see variously a bow and arrow, a crossbow, flying fish, harp, bridge, tower, bird, airplane, or many other things.

In designing the work, Morrel said that "form, rather than the concept, dominated the process." One might add that form also has taken over the process of perceiving the piece. Like the earlier sculptures, *Pilot Bridge* is participatory: one climbs the stairway to stand within the structure. Being in the work itself is central to the process of association its ambiguous forms demand: by climbing the stairs one is literally suspended between corporeal reality—symbolized by the granite boulder below—and the higher realm of aesthetic experience, a place where one's imagination is free to interact with the forms of the piece. The viewer, literally and figuratively, is at the center of the work; nothing in specific is given, and one's own imagination is preponderate in the experience. The "meaning" of *Pilot Bridge* is constructed from the interplay of its forms and one's own thoughts and feelings.

Ever since the completion of *Asylum,* 1978, Morrel has used drawing, photography and collage to pursue in two dimensions his interest in the act of perception. In the 1980s, such work has come to play an increasingly important role in his continuing development. These media have not displaced sculpture, but neither can they in any way be considered a secondary aspect of Morrel's production. Some of these works relate to a particular sculptural project, whether it be an existing work or a proposal for an unrealized one. Others, specifically some of the photo-collages, do not. None are ever intended as ersatz re-creations of sculptural experiences. Instead, they are more like translations: as in the sculpture, they undermine the conditioned patterns of perception, but they do so using a different language.

It was *Asylum* that sparked a new involvement with photography for Morrel. He had taken photographs since childhood, but had never seriously considered using it as a creative end in itself. He had made photographs of the earlier sculptures, but was interested only in documenting them; indeed the photographs he made of *Telescopic Reference Points, Desk Axis,* and *Catapult 70°* are the only existing visual records of these works. The first photographs of *Asylum* also may have been intended to be purely documentary, but he soon discovered that the details of his photographs revealed things in the work he had not seen before. At this point, he began to use photography more deliberately to explore these heretofore hidden aspects of the piece: "With *Asylum,* I fell in love with photography, and began to use it to intensely discover my own work, to discover new pieces within the work."

In photographing his sculpture, Morrel frequently singles out and intensifies an element within the work that closely corresponds to a specific sculptural idea. The composition of *Red Light,* 1978 (Cat. No. 8), for instance, echoes in a more exaggerated fashion the skewed, "neo-constructivist" structure of *Asylum.* Moreover, the rushing perspective of the photograph, a spatial distortion caused by the focal length of the lens, reiterates and heightens the tensions set up by the irregular angles of *Asylum's* construction. Another example, *City Mirror,* 1978 (Cat. No. 13), can be related to Morrel's interest in directing the attention of the viewer beyond the work itself toward the surrounding landscape. In this photograph, the mirrored wall of *Asylum* is virtually invisible as it is subsumed into a grand, indeed nearly sublime, vision of clouds at dusk. In viewing this work it is useful to remember that Morrel, speaking about *Asylum,* once told a reviewer that in ideal circumstances, "the piece becomes invisible."[7]

Photographs that initially seem purely documentary turn out not to be so on closer examination. *Third River,* 1980 (Cat. No. 16), at first appears to be a distant view of *Omega,* but another look reveals it to be a double exposure combining two different views. In a nearly seamless transition, Morrel juxtaposed the image of a nearby bridge with his sculpture; the effect is not unlike the abrupt shift in viewpoints Morrel obtains through the use of mirrors in the piece itself. The image of the bridge in association with *Omega* also enriches the photograph on a metaphorical level: it alludes to *Omega* as a "bridge" to new perceptual experiences, and at the same time, refers to the original suspension bridge that stood on the site.

Reflected images occupy an important position in Morrel's formal vocabulary. Their importance for his photographs and photo-collages is perhaps less evident than in the sculpture, yet they were instrumental in leading Morrel to develop the dynamic spatial arrangements characteristic of his finest photographs and collages. Morrel's interest in the photographic possibilities of reflected images can be seen as early as 1978, in his first "mature" photographs of *Asylum.* In one of these works (Cat. No. 9), the edge of the mirrored wall where it joins a row of prison bars forms the vertical center of the image, so that one half of the picture is a reflection, while the other half is not. Although the bars and their reflection allow some continuity between the two halves, two views of the city appear from conflicting perspectives. By shooting into the mirror, Morrel was able to "cut up the piece": in effect, "to do a piece on the piece." The technique was refined in later works such as *Splitting,* 1980 and *McGraw-Hill Rising,* 1982 (cover illustration). Soon after *Asylum,* he began photographing other subjects besides his sculpture, and he manipulated the image by holding a mirror in front of the lens. Wanting to obtain even more abrupt shifts in perspective and unusual juxtapositions of forms, he moved from cutting up the image with a mirror to cutting up and rearranging parts of the photographs themselves. By 1981, Morrel had made enough large-scale collages of such refinement and complexity that they constituted a whole new category within his oeuvre.

Compositionally, the collages range from symmetrical, relatively simple combinations of as few as two "mirror" images to dynamic assemblies of a multitude of interpenetrating forms. Among the former is a particularly elegant untitled work from 1982 (Cat. No. 55). The ostensible subject of the collage is a power station; in the photograph on which it is based, Morrel split the image with a mirror, so that the forms appear alongside and at a right angle to their reflections. To assemble the collage, Morrel printed the photograph twice, once in reverse, and placed the two prints side-by-side, juxtaposing the original photograph with its mirror image. At the opposite end of the spectrum is an untitled collage of 1981 (Cat. No. 62). It is among Morrel's most abstract works; only the presence of steel beams connect it to reality and keep it from drifting over into total non-objectivity. Composed of a number of acutely angled planes fitted together in an eccentrically-shaped whole, the work is a virtuoso display of staccato visual rhythms. As one scans the work, the eye is led from one section to another by the lines of the steel beams, but there are so many interruptions, reversals, stops and starts, that a smooth and continuous reading of the overall image is impossible. The experience is analogous to that of the sculpture: in both cases, Morrel employs various means to shatter ordinary appearances, so that viewers are forced to see familiar things from a new perspective.

In many of the collages, Morrel drew ruled lines that extend the planes of the collage elements out into the surrounding space. These linear elements play a compositional role by tying the disparate, fragmented views together, in effect, "locking" the planes in place. They also direct a viewer's attention along certain lines of sight, suggesting spatial recession and establishing the boundaries of planes into which the collage elements are fitted. Understood as sightlines, they recall the invisible sightlines that defined the boundaries of *Telescopic Reference Points.* Yet, the lines in the collages are never allowed to establish a consistent pictorial perspective; the viewer is constantly forced to readjust his or her point of view by the conflicting perspectives established by the planar forms. A particularly interesting use of linear elements in a collage is found in *Boomerang,* 1982 (Cat. No. 26), so titled because of the appearance of the sculpture in the work. Near the bottom center of the image, a number of lines converge toward an imaginary vanishing point, becoming fainter as they do so to increase the illusion of spatial recession. However, the conventional one-point perspective established by the lines is not adhered to by the photographic elements. Embedded within the "rational" space of the perspective lines, they present alternate or conflicting viewpoints. The sense of colliding perspectives is emphasized by the left center of the image, where the collage assumes the form of a wedge-shaped arrow, which appears to pass through the "solid" plane of a building facade.

The appearance of *Boomerang* in this and other collages underscores the fact that the sculptures and the collages are linked by a common set of intentions: in both Morrel seeks to free perception from its dependence on habit and restore imagination to the way we see. When a sculpture makes an appearance in a collage, it functions like a key to the experience, a touchstone around which the drama of the collage unfolds and ultimately refers. The relationship between the sculpture and the collages is especialy evident in another collage work related to *Boomerang* (Cat. No. 29). In this work, the sculpture appears in place near the top of the McGraw-Hill building. The shape of the image as a whole echoes the wing shape of the sculpture. The building is shown from two different viewpoints that are at right angles to one another and are joined together in such an effective manner that they appear to share a common face. As a result, the two views coalesce to give the appearance of a single edifice, which with its attached "wings," seems somehow to be flying through space. The allusion to flight, as already noted, was a major part of the experience of the sculpture.

Drawing has played a double-sided role in Morrel's work, serving both as a way to work out sculptural ideas, and with greater frequency in recent years, as an independent end in itself. Morrel has always drawn, but he never pursued it with the same sense of purpose as in the sculpture until the end of the 1970s. In the early sculptures he had worked "direct": drawing played only a minor role in the development of a particular piece. *"Asylum,"* he notes, "was drawn on the back of a napkin." In 1979, he made a number of drawings—some on photographs—for an unrealized project, a bridge between the roofs of two skyscrapers. Coming after *Asylum,* the bridge project has many affinities with the earlier piece, particularly in the use of two mirrored walls with doors through which one would pass in crossing the bridge. The style of the drawings recalls the eccentric geometry of the sculptures.

Morrel made a number of drawings for *Omega* and *Boomerang,* showing the works from different angles as if he wanted to work out every aspect of their appearance before their actual construction. Yet not all of these are "studies" of the kind we usually associate with sculptors' drawings. In a drawing of *Omega* (Cat. No. 20), drawn with the aid of a computer, Morrel elaborated the image with colored pencil lines that appear to emanate from the structure. *Omega* thus is made to seem as if it possesses some sort of latent radiant energy. Another drawing, a 1980 study for *Boomerang* (Cat. No. 23), has a similar effect; the boomerang shape occupies the center of the image, and is the focus of a series of rectilinear planes which radiate out from the central core. It might be said that the drawing to an extent is an attempt to anticipate the experience of the sculpture: with its dynamic planar movement and rushing perspective, the drawing reads like the visual equivalent of vertigo.

Within the past three years, Morrel's drawings have become increasingly refined; at the same time, they have grown in scale. Morrel's vision has always been expansive, so it is not unexpected that his drawings would grow in size as he became more adept at handling the medium. At this point (Summer, 1984), drawings nine feet high are not uncommon. Most of the recent drawings are related to sculptural projects, either to the recently constructed *Pilot Bridge* (Cat. No. 31), or to several unrealized projects: *Pharos* (Cat. No. 43), *Ankor,* and *Satellite* (Cat. No. 46). Formally, the projects are all closely related, and if they are ever realized—perhaps it should be said *when* they are realized—they will constitute a series of works of which *Pilot Bridge* is the beginning. That Morrel is able to develop an entire series of works on paper prior to their actual realization points to the fact that in Morrel's thinking, the power of the work as an image, that is, its power to function as an open-ended metaphor, has assumed as much importance as the experience of the sculpture itself had previously. A drawing of *Ankor* (Cat. No. 41), is loaded with allusions that might serve as a guide to the imagery of all the new proposed works. The reference to a bow and arrow, and the tension between them as the bow is stretched taut, relates to flight. There is also a sexual allusion, fairly obvious, in the arrow which pierces another in the center. Finally, the whole piece is embedded in a granite boulder, which as in *Pilot Bridge,* is symbolic of the earth, of being bound to the earth by the force of gravity. Clearly, like the sculptures, Morrel thinks of his drawings as vehicles: the one for flights of perceptual experience, the other for flights of the imagination.

Owen Morrel's work, his "mature" work, began less than a decade ago; most of his career still lies ahead. Yet to measure his accomplishments over the past eight years and to place his work within the context of contemporary sculpture is to see the utter originality of his approach. He has participated in the trend toward viewer interactive site work, and in the move away from non-objectivity to open-ended, "literary" content. Yet unlike many site-specific sculptors who choose to place their works in natural surroundings—where they will not have to compete with the noise and activity of the urban environment—Morrel has not hesitated to locate his work in the city, indeed to even make the city and its architecture work for him. Morrel often talks as if he were creating sanctuaries for jaded city dwellers rather than sculptures; he speaks of wanting to "altar" the city's skyline, of creating works which lift us above our ordinary environment and catalyze our desires for psychological liberation. It is this exaltation of the viewer's experience, and Morrel's ability to use personal expression as a springboard into the realm of the universal, that is perhaps his most important contribution to contemporary art . . . so far.

Trent Myers

1. *Telescopic Reference Points,* 1976

2. *Telescopic Reference Points*, 1976

6. *Catapult 70°*, 1977

10. *Asylum*, 1978

13. *City Mirror,* 1978

15. *Red Riding,* (Omega) 1980

24. *Boomerang,* 1981

26. *Boomerang*, 1982

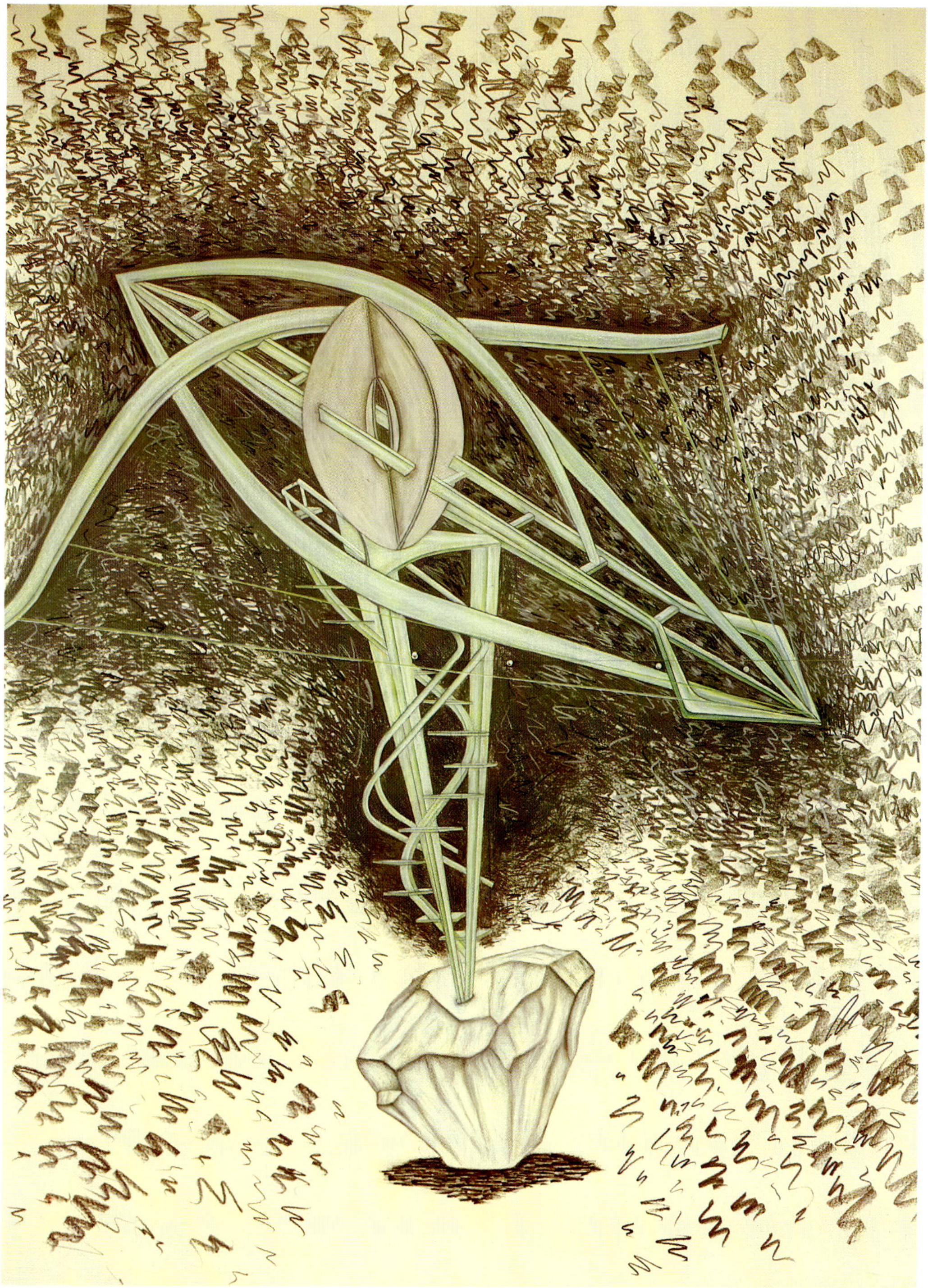

31. *Pilot Bridge,* 1983

35. *Pilot Bridge*, 1984

4. *Desk Axis,* 1976

8. *Red Light*, 1978

9. *Asylum,* 1978

16. *Third River*, 1980

17. *The Hanged Man,* 1980

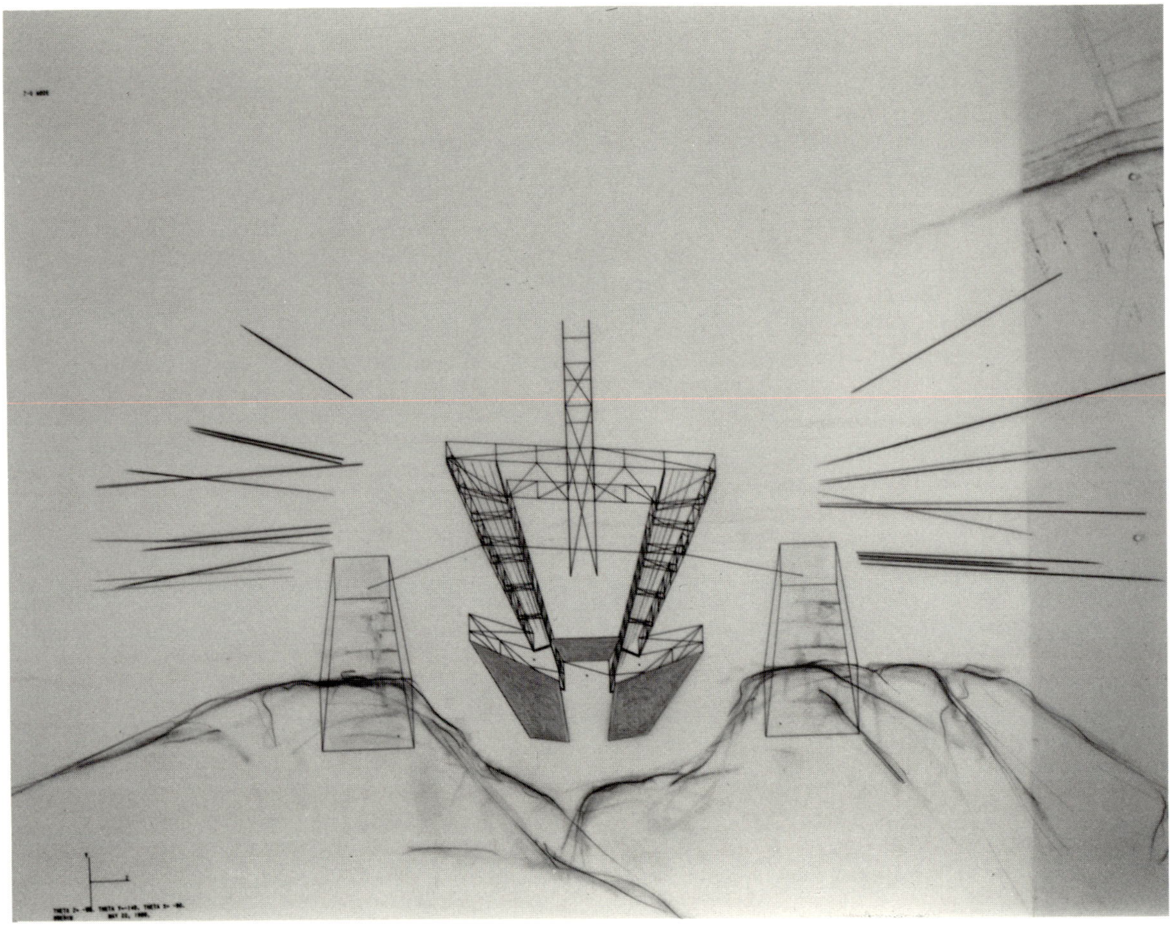

20. *Omega*, 1980 (detail)

23. *Boomerang*, 1980

27. *Boomerang,* 1981

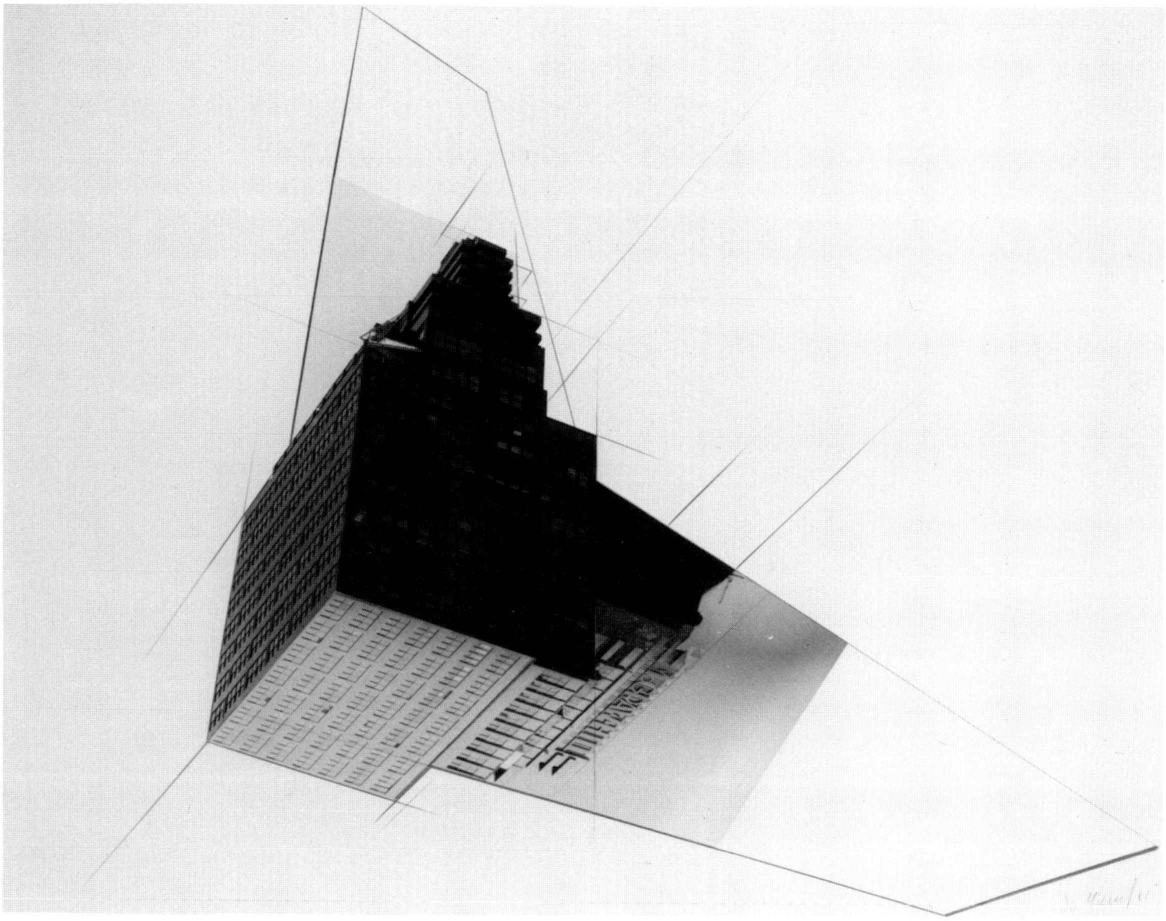

29. *Untitled,* 1981

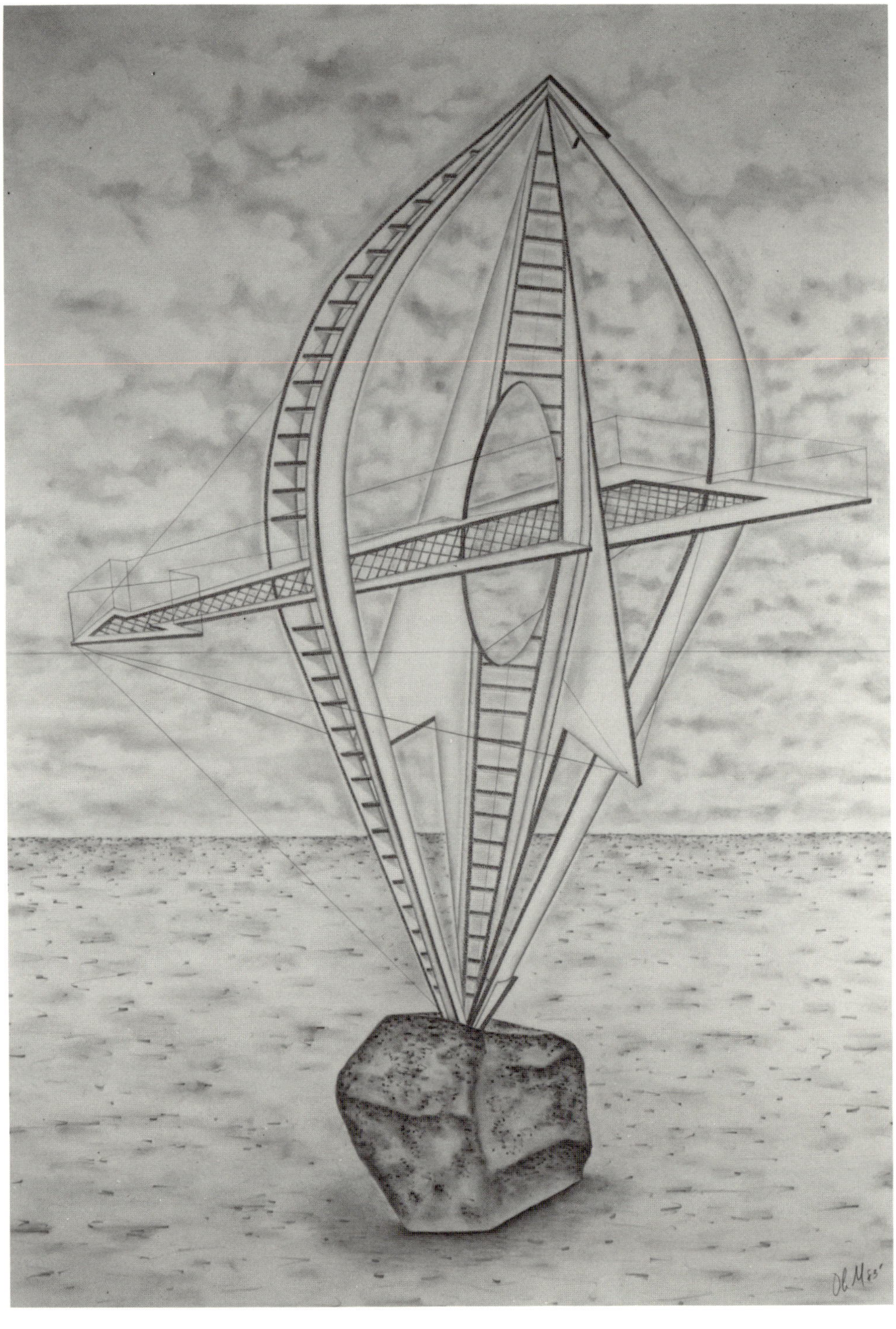

41. *Study For Ankor,* 1983

43. *Pharos,* 1982

55. *Untitled,* 1982

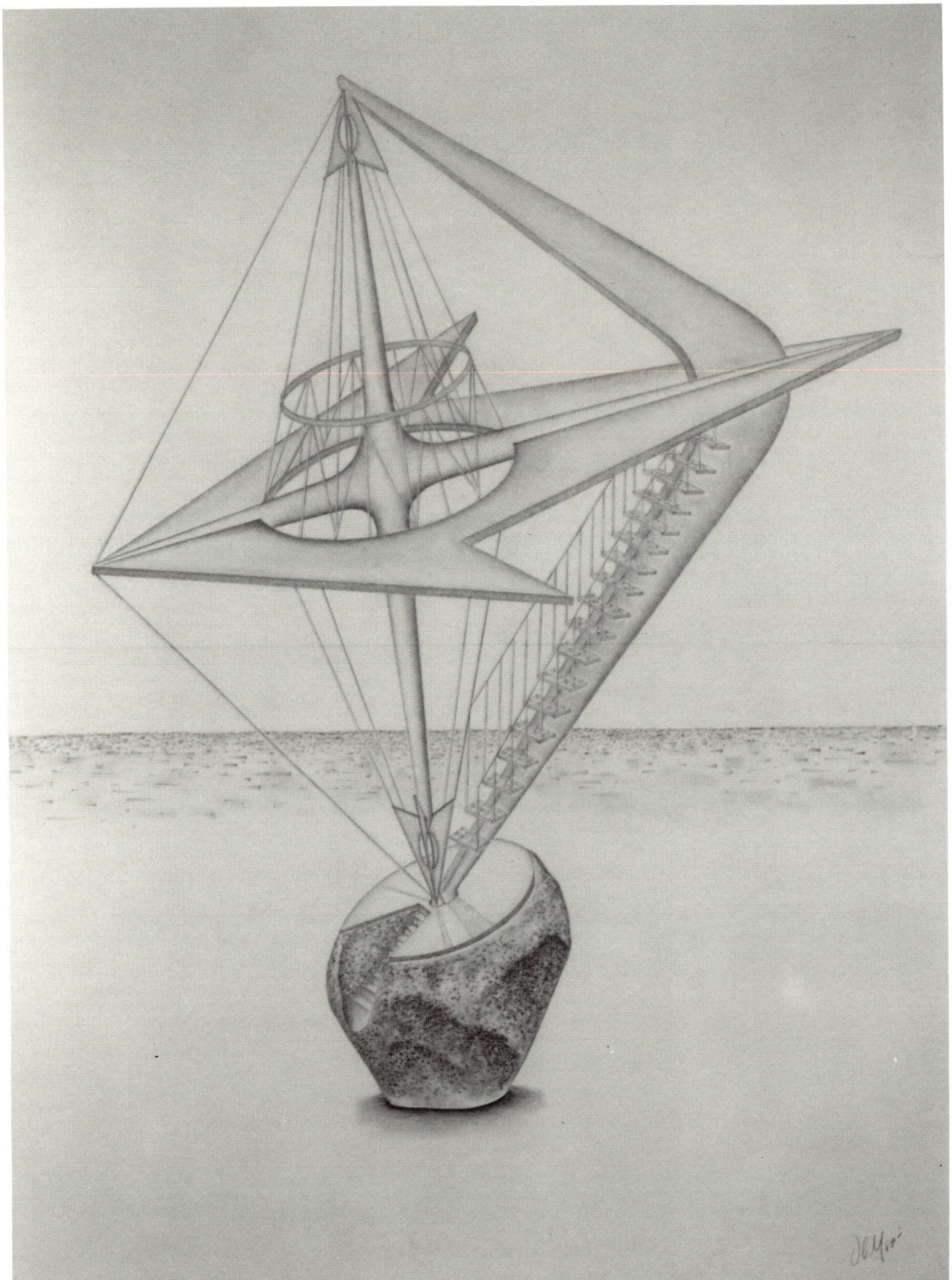

46. *Satellite,* 1984

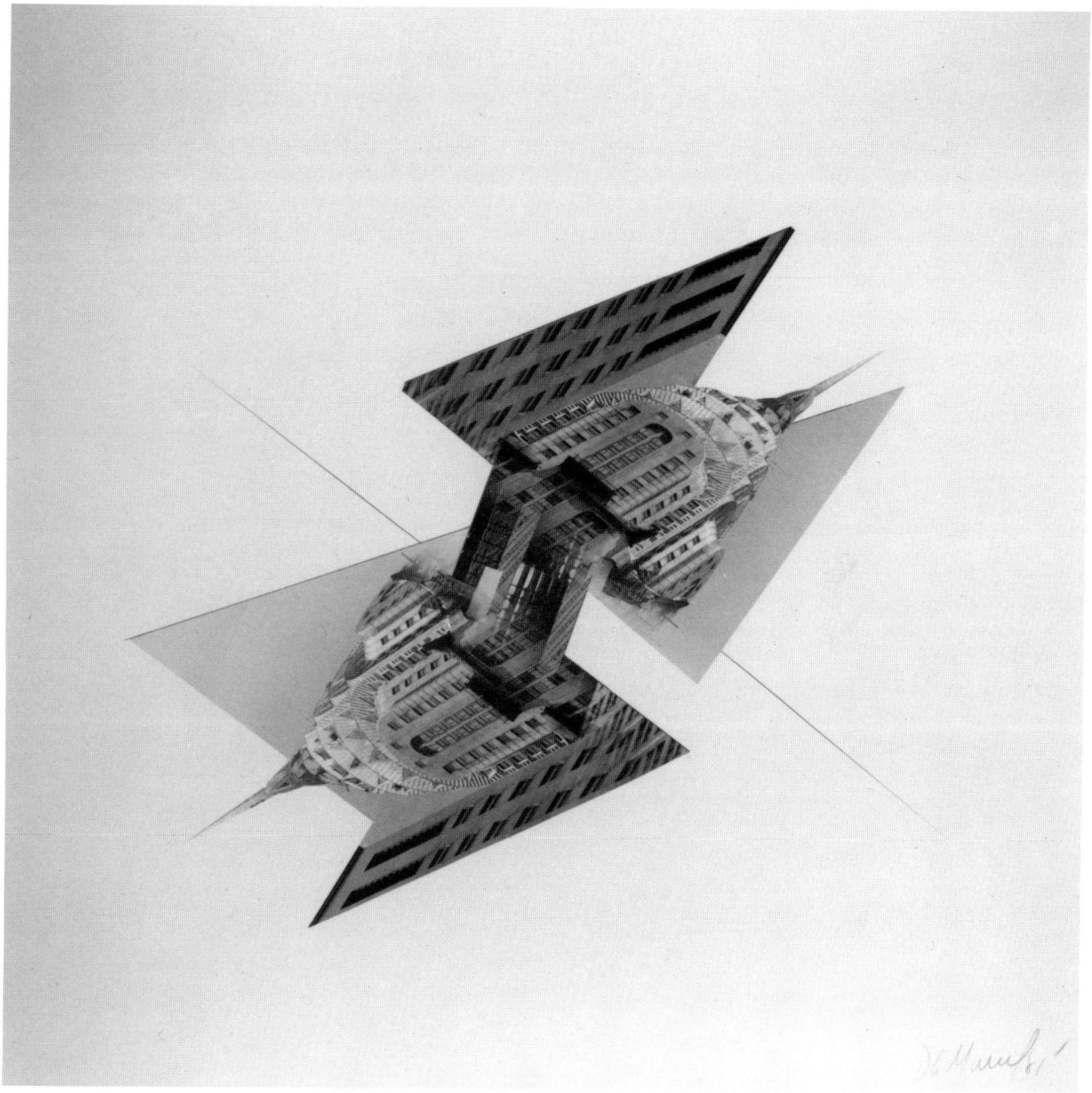

57. *Untitled,* 1981

59. *Untitled*, 1982

61. *Cathedral*, 1981

62. *Untitled*, 1981

Catalog of the Exhibition

Unless otherwise indicated, all works are collection the artist. Height precedes width precedes depth.

1. *Telescopic Reference Points,* 1976
cibachrome photograph
40″ x 30″

2. *Telescopic Reference Points,* 1976
cibachrome photograph
30″ x 40″

3. *Nine to Five,* 1976
cibachrome photograph
30″ x 40″

4. *Desk Axis,* 1976
cibachrome photograph
30″ x 40″

5. *World Desk,* 1976
cibachrome photograph
26-3/4″ x 39″

6. *Catapult 70°,* 1977
cibachrome photograph
27-1/2″ x 39-1/2″
Collection Charles L. Zarett, New York

7. *Fade Away,* 1978
cibachrome photograph
25-1/4″ x 38-1/2″

8. *Red Light,* 1978
cibachrome photograph
25-1/4″ x 36-1/4″

9. *Asylum,* 1978
cibachrome photograph
30″ x 40″

10. *Asylum,* 1978
cibachrome photograph
30″ x 40″

11. *Maya,* 1978
cibachrome photograph
30″ x 40″

12. *Asylum,* 1978
cibachrome photograph
26-1/2″ x 39″

13. *City Mirror,* 1978
cibachrome photograph
30″ x 40″
Collection Charles L. Zarett, New York

14. *Asylum,* 1978
(maquette)
bronze, copper, wood and glass
25″ x 31″ x 31″
Collection Mr. and Mrs. Scott Hodes, Chicago

15. *Red Riding,* 1980
cibachrome photograph
26-3/4″ x 38″

16. *Third River,* 1980
cibachrome photograph
20″ x 24″

17. *The Hanged Man,* 1980
cibachrome photograph
38-1/4″ x 26″

18. *Splitting,* 1980
cibachrome photograph
40″ x 30″

19. *Omega,* 1980
ink, graphite and colored pencil on tracing paper
34-1/2″ x 56″
Collection Charles L. Zarett, New York

20. *Omega,* 1980
ink, graphite and colored pencil on tracing paper with blueprint
35″ x 62″
Collection Madison Art Center, Gift of Scott Hodes

21. *Omega,* 1980
(maquette)
bronze, copper, wood and glass
16″ x 18″ x 28″
Collection Louis Gaudiosi, New York

22. *Study for Boomerang,* 1980
graphite and crayon on paper
22″ x 30″

23. *Boomerang,* 1980
graphite on paper
25″ x 22-1/2″

24. *Boomerang,* 1981
cibachrome photograph
24″ x 20″

25. *Boomerang,* 1981
cibachrome photograph
20″ x 16″

26. *Boomerang,* 1982
photo-collage and graphite
35-3/4″ x 38-1/2″

27. *Boomerang,* 1981
photo-collage and graphite
70″ x 50″

28. *McGraw-Hill Rising,* 1981
cibachrome photograph
40″ x 30″

29. *Untitled,* 1981
photo-collage and graphite
38-1/4″ x 50″

30. *Boomerang,* 1982
(maquette)
bronze, copper, wood and glass
25″ x 11″ x 8″
Collection Louis Gaudiosi, New York

31. *Pilot Bridge,* 1983
crayon and graphite on paper
86″ x 61″

32. *Study for Pilot Bridge,* 1983
graphite on paper
14″ x 17″

33. *Pilot Bridge,* 1983
(maquette)
steel, bronze and granite
66″ x 43″ x 36″
Lent Anonymously

34. *Pilot Bridge,* 1983
graphite on paper
59″ x 43″

35. *Pilot Bridge,* 1984
cibachrome photograph
24″ x 20″

36. *Pilot Bridge,* 1984
cibachrome photograph
24″ x 20″

37. *Pilot Bridge,* 1984
cibachrome photograph
24″ x 20″

38. *Pilot Bridge,* 1984
cibachrome photograph
24″ x 20″

39. *Ankor,* 1983
graphite on paper
14″ x 18″

40. *Ankor,* 1983
graphite on paper
61″ x 43″

41. *Study for Ankor,* 1983
graphite on paper
31″ x 22″

42. *Ankor,* 1984
(maquette)
aluminum and granite
144″ x 84″ x 34″

43. *Pharos,* 1982
graphite on paper
44″ x 35-1/2″

44. *Pharos,* 1982
pastel and graphite on paper
30″ x 22-1/4″

45. *Pharos,* 1981
graphite on paper
113″ x 50″

46. *Satellite,* 1984
graphite on paper
61″ x 43″

47. *Satellite,* 1984
graphite and colored pencil on paper
60-1/2″ x 43″

48. *Untitled* (Study for Bridge Project), 1979
collage and graphite on paper
23-1/8″ x 29-1/8″

49. *Untitled* (Study for Bridge Project), 1979
2 parts
graphite on gray paper with mirrored mylar
each part, 19-1/2″ x 25-1/4″

50. *Untitled* (Study for Bridge Project), 1979
colored pencil on mylar
22-1/4″ x 30″

51. *Satellite,* 1982
photo-collage
27″ x 22″

52. *Untitled,* 1982
photo-collage
27″ x 22-1/2″

53. *Untitled,* 1982
photo-collage
22″ x 30″

54. *Untitled,* 1982
photo-collage and graphite
30″ x 22″

55. *Untitled,* 1982
photo-collage
22-1/2″ x 30″

56. *Untitled,* 1982
photo-collage, graphite and colored pencil
74″ x 50″

57. *Untitled,* 1981
photo-collage
37-3/4″ x 38-1/4″

58. *City Rocket,* 1981
photo-collage
52″ x 64″

59. *Untitled,* 1982
photo-collage
32″ x 38″

60. *Untitled,* 1982
photo-collage
50″ x 38″

61. *Cathedral,* 1981
photo-collage
49-1/2″ x 76-1/4″

62. *Untitled,* 1981
photo-collage
79″ x 58″

63. *Untitled* (Study for Bridge Project), 1978
2 parts
ink on mylar over photograph, 9-5/8″ x 13-1/2″
photograph, 6-5/8″ x 9-1/2″

64. *Rocket,* 1980
crayon, colored pencil and graphite on paper
22-1/2″ x 30″

Exhibitions and Installations

Born: Long Island, New York, 1950
Education: Colgate University, Hamilton, New York;
Cranbrook Academy of Art, Bloomfield Hills, Michigan;
Skidmore College, Saratoga Springs, New York.

1975
Telescopic Tree, New York City.

1976
Telescopic Reference Points, Poughkeepsie, New York.
Desk Axis, New York City.

1977
Catapult 70°, New York City.

1978
Asylum, New York City.

1979
Galerie Yvon Lambert, Paris.
Galerie Alfred Schmela, Düsseldorf.

1980
Omega, Artpark, Lewiston, New York.
Galerie Yvon Lambert, Paris.
Galerie Ugo Ferranti, Rome.
Galerie Francoise Lambert, Milan.

1981
1981 Biennial Exhibition, Whitney Museum of American Art, New York City.
Boomerang, New York City.
Bonlow Gallery, New York City.

1984
Pilot Bridge, New York City.
Ted Greenwald Gallery, New York City.

All exhibitions listed are one-person shows with the exception of the 1981 Whitney Biennial.

Bibliography

1976

Bourdon, David. "Owen Morrel Makes Optical Allusions," *Village Voice,* December 13, p. 109.

1977

Bourdon, David. "An Artist Sees Far," *Du,* pp. 9-10.

Brunelle, Al. "Owen Morrel in Poughkeepsie and New York," *Art in America,* July/August, pp. 93-94.

Levin, Kim. "Owen Morrel," *Arts Magazine,* February, p. 14.

1978

Anderson, Alexandra. "Owen Morrel," *Village Voice,* July 24, p. 47.

Ashbery, John. "Asylum in the Sky," *New York Magazine,* August 28, pp. 103-104.

Cavaliere, Barbara. "Cityworks," *Arts Magazine,* November, p. 19.

"Ein Gefangnis Diensie Der Freiheit," *Du,* September, pp. 26-27.

Glueck, Grace. "Sculpture Under a City Sky," *New York Times,* July 14, p. C-23.

________________. "Art People," *New York Times,* July 21, p. C-18.

Kingsley, April. "Revisionism," *Village Voice,* September 25, p. 113.

Marzoratti, Gerrald. "Museum Without Walls," *Soho Weekly News,* July 27, p. 20.

Perlberg, Deborah. "Reviews: New York," *Artforum,* December, pp. 65-66.

1979

Miller, Larry. "Art in New York," *Paletten,* April, pp. 2-11.

Nadelman, Cynthia. "What's that forest doing in Greenwich Village?", *ARTnews,* November, pp. 66-71.

1980

"Artpark 1980," Lewiston, New York: Artpark, pp. 25-28.

Ashbery, John. "Two For The Road," *New York Magazine,* July 28, pp. 52-53.

Cavaliere, Barbara. "The Making of 'Omega'," *Arts Magazine,* October, pp. 118-122.

Friedricks, Y. "Galerie Schmela, Düsseldorf; Ausstellung," *Kunstwerk,* 33, no 2, pp. 75-76.

Larson, Kay. "Is There a Crimp in the Beauty Parlor?", *Village Voice,* September 10, p. 77.

McFadden, Sarah. "Going Places, Part II: The Outside Story," *Art in America,* Summer, pp. 51-61.

________________. "Reflections on a Tilted Ramp," *Art in America,* November, pp. 120-123.

McKinnon, Michael. *Art of the 1970s* (filmstrip). History of Western Art. London: Visual Publications International, p. 9.

Marzoratti, Gerrald. "Outa Site," *Soho Weekly News,* June 25, p. 37.

Trebay, Guy. "Struts and Hums," *Village Voice,* July 23, p. 52.

Volz, Wolfgang. "Omega" (photo-essay), *Plus,* October 29, pp. 26-28.

Anonymous. "New Sight at Niagara," *Der Spiegel,* July 14, p. 137.

1981

Anderson, Alexandra. "Vignettes," *Portfolio,* November/December, p. 8.

Glueck, Grace. "Tracking the Marvelous," *New York Times,* April 24, p. C-19.

Nuridsany, Michel. "Asylum and Omega," *Art Press,* February, p. 18.

"1981 Biennial Exhibition," New York: Whitney Museum of American Art, p. 79.

Anonymous. "Omega e Niagara," *Domus,* February, p. 56.

1982

Ashbery, John. "Don't Look Down," *Newsweek,* February 1, p. 77.

Castle, Ted and Michals, Duane. "Art in its Place," *Geo Magazine,* September, pp. 64-67.

Gorgoni, Gianfranco. "Boomerang," *Actuel Magazine,* February, pp. 34-35.

Karmel, Pepe. "Photography: Urban Disjunctions," *Art in America,* March, pp. 45-49.

Larson, Kay. "On Edge," *New York Magazine,* January, pp. 64-65.

Pearlman, Jill. "Boomerang," *Us,* April 27, pp. 22-23. pp. 22-23.

Tomkins, Calvin. "Boomerang," *The New Yorker,* April 19, pp. 36-37.

1984

Brenson, Michael. "Sculpture Goes Outdoors," *New York Times,* July 13, p. C-20.

Christo, C. "Le Toucher de l'espace et du Temps," *Artistes,* March, pp. 18-20.

Notes to the Introduction

1. Quoted in Barbara Cavaliere, ''The Making of Omega,'' *Arts Magazine,* October, 1980, p. 120. Unless otherwise indicated, all remarks by the artist were made in conversation with the author in the spring of 1984.
2. For more on the gradual disappearance of the sculptural base in 20th century art, see Jack Burnham, *Beyond Modern Sculpture* (New York: George Braziller, Inc., 1968).
3. The phrase is Rosalind Kraus's. See Rosalind Kraus, ''Sculpture in the Expanded Field,'' *October,* 8 (Spring, 1979), 30-44.
4. Quoted in Cavaliere, *op. cit.,* p. 118.
5. Sarah McFadden, ''Reflections on a Tilted Ramp,'' *Art in America,* November, 1980, p. 123.
6. Cavaliere's article is an excellent account of the collaborative process in the building of *Omega, op. cit.,* pp. 118-122.
7. See Cynthia Nadelman, ''What's that forest doing in Greenwich Village?'', *ARTnews,* November, 1979, p. 70.

Photography Credits
Owen Morrel, Cat. Nos. 27, 1, 2, 4, 10, 15, 24, 35, 8, 13, 16, 9, 62, 26, 29.
Howard Greenberg, Cat. No. 6.
Maurice Thaler, Cat. Nos. 55, 20, 23, 43, 46, 57, 17, 61, 59.
Zendeman/Fremont, Cat. Nos. 31, 41.

Madison Art Center Staff

Thomas H. Garver, Director

Curatorial
Janet Ela, Curator of Collections
Peg Koetsch, Curator of Education and Public Programming
Trent Myers, Curator of Exhibitions
Robert F. Schroeder, Registrar

Administrative
Clay Bacon, Bookkeeper/Accountant
Amy Grimm, Gallery Shop Manager
James Kramer, Security
William Lindemann, Technical Services Supervisor
Pam McDonald, Security
Roxanne Olsen, Security
Michael J. Paggie, Business Manager
Marina Rodriquez, Gallery Shop Assistant
Barbara Scherz, Membership and Program Liaison
Kathy Silbiger, Assistant Director for Development and Community Relations
Sharon Reilly Williams, Receptionist

Part-time
Barry Carlsen, Technical Services Assistant
Kiersten Foget, Gallery Shop Assistant
Nate Griese, Security
Deborah Jahn, Development Assistant
Neil Rickman, Security
Barbara Seffrood, Typist
Royce Weatherly, Technical Services Assistant
Louise Weinberg, Curatorial Assistant
Gwen Winston, Typist

Photography Credits
Maurice Thaler

Board of Trustees